THE STORY BEHIND THE POEM

THE STORY BEHIND the POEM

A reflection on mommyhood, miscarriages & marriage

AMY OSELKIN

The Story Behind the Poem: A Reflection on Mommyhood, Miscarriages and Marriage
Copyright © 2022 by Amy Oselkin

All rights reserved
No portion of this book may be reproduced, stored in a retrieval system, or transmitted in any form by any means–electronic, mechanical, photocopy, recording, or other–except for brief quotations in printed reviews, without prior permission of the author.

First Edition

Paperback ISBN:979-8-9873477-0-6
Hardcover ISBN: 979-8-9873477-1-3
eBook ISBN: 979-8-9873477-2-0

To my husband,
who gave me the idea for this book and
continues to love me after all these years
To my parents, family and friends,
who always support and believe in me
And especially to my children,
who inspire and amaze me everyday

TABLE OF CONTENTS

Preface	**ix**
Baby	**1**
Baby Fever	3
Dear Baby Owen	5
The Dishes and the Laundry Can Wait	7
How Much Longer Will I Be Here	9
Big Boy Dylan	13
Just One More	15
Miscarriages	**17**
Some Other Day	19
Miscarriage Part 1	21
Miscarriage Part 2	25
New News	27
What Comes After the Worst	29
Totally Undone	31
Birthday	33
The Hand I Never Held	35
A Year Later	37
Pregnancy	**39**
Introducing Pregnancy	41
My Little Seed	43
The Downside of Pregnancy	45
The Upside of Pregnancy	47
Mothering on a Prayer	49
Kaboom	51
Something New	53
Worthwhile	55

Relationships and Marriage	**57**
Martin	59
Blended	61
American Idol Song: As I Go Away	63
After I Do	67
The Doctor's Wife	69
Long Distance	73
Can't Relate	75
Divorce	77
Leaves Me Bitter	79
Little Surprises	81
Conclusion	**83**
About the Author	**85**

Dear Reader,

I am so excited to start this journey with you. I've been writing poems my entire life, but the idea for this book came from my husband, Martin, a few years ago. He has always been a huge supporter of my writing and encouraged me to gather all the poems together and not just publish them, but also tell readers the story behind the poem. So, after every poem, I include a little context into what was going on in my life and a photo from that time period.

Just to give you my background, I am from Los Angeles, CA. If you have ever seen the movie *Clueless*, I truly am a "Valley girl." However, I've lived in Atlanta, Manhattan, Brooklyn, Philadelphia and now reside in Allentown, PA. My husband and I met when we were nineteen years old at Emory University in Atlanta, Georgia and have been together ever since. We have two boys, Dylan, nine, and Owen, five, and our little girl, Danika Lily, two. For the past ten years, I've been selling Clarks shoes live on QVC. I love it! I grew up watching QVC so to be on-air there is a dream come true. Previously, I was the Senior Lifestyle Editor at *In Touch Weekly* where I wrote about celebrity fashion, beauty, fitness, weddings and plastic surgery. I even got to cover the royal wedding of William and Kate and New York Fashion Week. Plus, I snuck in some free Botox. It was a great gig. Before that, I was an intern, production assistant and ultimately a field producer for *E! News* in both LA and NYC. The highlight was covering Tom Cruise and Katie Holmes' wedding in Italy and yes, I was bummed, but not that surprised, it didn't work out. *Wow*, as I am writing this, I am thinking, this sounds impressive, but trust me, I paid my dues. Before *E! News*, I was a page at CBS where my responsibilities included seating the audience at *American Idol* and asking them to spit their chewing gum in my plastic cup!

I truly am an open book, and I hope by reading these poems you find comfort and a friend.

Amy Dulkin

Baby

Dylan was conceived the night this photo was taken.

BABY FEVER
November 2012

You haven't even been conceived, and yet I already love you
I envision your hair and eyes, singing you lullabies
You haven't even been conceived, and yet I already love you
I dream about your smile
If you'll walk fast or take a while
Will you look like me or your handsome dad
Whoever it is, I'll be so glad
We want to hold you and comfort you right away
We will shower you with love every single day
You will be the best gift on earth
I can't wait until your birth.

Story behind the poem
It's so amazing to read this poem now, as Dylan is nine years old, and know the answers to the questions I presented. Dylan walked at fourteen months, looks like me and truly is the best gift. Dylan wasn't even conceived until seven months after I wrote this poem, but it shows that I wanted him for so long.

Owen at five months old.

DEAR BABY OWEN
January 18, 2018

Even though I pee a bit every time I jump
And look like I still have a four-month baby bump
I see your perfect nose, full cheeks and pursed lips
And thank G-d for this miracle that permanently expanded my hips
Yes, my once perky breasts are now droopy
But I love every inch of you, even your poopy
Sure, I wonder if my jeans will ever fit
And if we can get through just one feeding without spit
But every morning when you smile up at me
I feel warm, happy and truly blessed to be your mommy.

Story behind the poem

I wrote this late at night while watching my second son, Owen, sleeping. I should have been sleeping too but he looked so adorable I couldn't take it. This is the first poem I wrote about Owen. The love I feel for him every day is completely consuming. I'm so grateful my heart delightfully expanded, I just wish my body would shrink back.

I believe the best feeling in the world is when my child sleeps on me.

THE DISHES AND THE LAUNDRY CAN WAIT
May 2018

The dishes and the laundry can wait
Because before I know it, you're gonna graduate
You'll be crossing that stage and I'll be sitting in the bleachers
Crying and clapping with other parents and teachers
Days like today will slip away too soon. I know they will
So I'm just gonna hold you and rock you and beg time to stand still
Please understand, I want you to grow and be the man you are destined to
But for today you are my precious baby and I'm going to spoil you
So the phone can keep ringing and toys can be all over the place
Because all I'm meant to do right now is memorize your tiny face
The love I have for you is beyond compare
It started as a seed and now it's blossomed everywhere
I'm so grateful for these golden afternoons just cradling you in my lap
And watching you as you slowly wake up from your nap
These moments are all priceless treasures to me
That I'll cherish forever as I watch you along your journey.

Story behind the poem
I wrote this poem when Owen was six months old. My friend Liana called me to tell me her daughter was graduating from high school this week and she was busy planning a graduation party. As we were talking, I was watching Owen rolling around on the floor and then it struck me that in a blink of an eye he would be all grown up. I looked around the house and instead of cleaning up or answering emails, I just scooped him up and held him tight. It was a perfect day.

Adorable photo of my boys taken on Purim 2019.

HOW MUCH LONGER WILL I BE HERE
December 22, 2018

Will I die before you're a man
How many more times can I hold your hand
Even when I'm gone will you keep me near
How much longer will I be here
So many things left to see
But G-d makes the plans and this is how he wants it to be
How much longer will I be here
You are special, there is no one like you
Try to accomplish everything you want to
How much longer will I be here
Be brave and be strong
Don't get upset when things go wrong
Listen to your heart but use your head
Please remember all the things I've said
I'm sorry I'm not always going to be here

I love you.

Story behind the poem

Dylan came to my room at 3:00 a.m. I was in a deep sleep. I came home from work late and hadn't slept much the night before. He wouldn't go back to his bed and wanted to watch TV. I let him. As I looked at his profile in the middle of the night, I thought: How much longer will I be here to watch him grow? How many more nights will I have like this? As tired as I was, I was happy to be with him and sadly I realized the day would come when I wouldn't be. A lot of my friends have lost their parents at a young age and I'm getting older and I hope I leave my kids with the right tools to live after I'm gone. And to give credit where credit is due, I love Tim McGraw's song "Humble and Kind" written by Lori McKenna. This poem has a similar quality so Tim, if you're up for recording this poem too, give me a call.

My favorite photo of Dylan at nearly three years-old in our yard in Philadelphia.

BIG BOY DYLAN
September 2017

Last night I kept staring at my son
Taking in his perfection, marveling at what he's become
Everything he does amazes me
Talking for hours, singing on key
How did we create such a masterpiece
The daily gifts you grant me, may they never cease.

Story behind the poem
I don't write enough about how amazing my son is or how much love I feel inside every time I look at him. How did I get so lucky to be his mom? Sure, like every kid, he has his moments, but overall his incredible spirit, mind and brilliance blow me away.

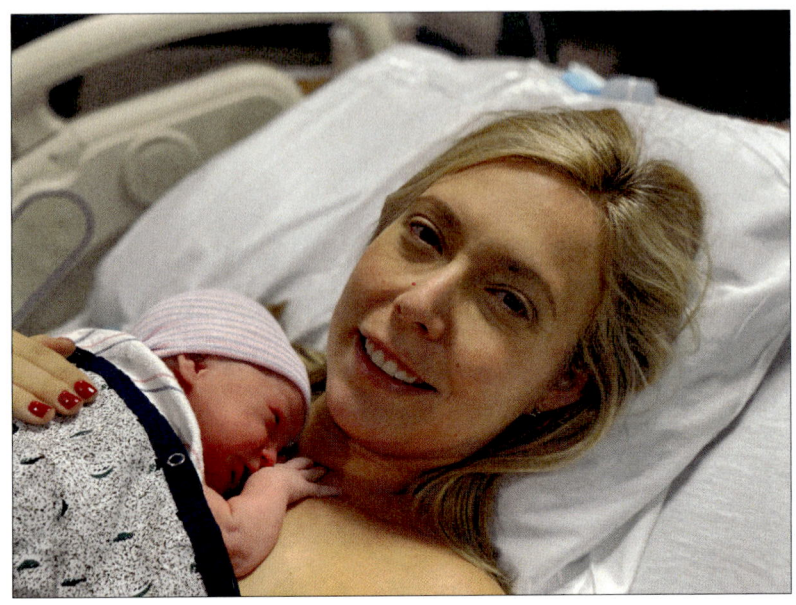

Princess Danika Lily has arrived. October 12, 2020.

JUST ONE MORE
March 26, 2019

I want a baby, just one more
I'm not ready to close the door
All the signs are saying we have enough
And adding another one will be beyond tough
But I wake up each day and feel someone is missing
There is one more forehead I'm meant to be kissing
I don't know if you feel the same
And creating a new life isn't a game
Once we commit, we are in it for the long run
But can you picture your life without another daughter or son?

Story behind the poem
I am sitting in my basement eating popcorn. My sons are asleep upstairs. My older son, Dylan, fractured a growth plate on his foot and is wearing a walking boot. My baby is snoring because he has a terrible cold. The days are long and stressful, and the nights are a gamble especially because Dylan hates going to sleep. And yet, with all the drama, I still want one more. I really do. I love my kids so much. I want just one more.

Update: I had a baby girl October 12, 2020. Dreams do come true. But the sleep deprivation is brutal.

Miscarriages

A pretty photo I took at Keukenhof Gardens in 2013. We started trying for a baby after this trip.

SOME OTHER DAY
June 9, 2013

I wasn't sure, but I was hoping you'd be there when I checked
But I was wrong and now I feel my dreams are wrecked
I pictured our lives together from day one
I'd hold you and take care of you until your worries were done
We'd figure things out together
Learning, growing forever
You'd be my special gift
All other priorities would shift
I'd protect you and lavish you in every way
So I'll just pray and wait to meet you some other day.

Story behind the poem

I was in Boston for work, and I took a pregnancy test in my hotel room and it came out negative. I was crushed. Martin and I started trying on May 28, 2013, and I really had a feeling I was pregnant. Then I went downstairs to meet my team for dinner and afterwards my boss and his boss were at the bar and told me that they didn't trust anyone until they took a tequila shot with them. So, I took a shot. This was a bit out of character for me since I'm not a big drinker. And then a few weeks later I took another pregnancy test, and I actually was pregnant. I just took the first test too early. I told Martin what happened, and he said it was OK because the kid was half Russian so he could take it.

We did a "reveal" for Dylan when we found out I was having a girl. Sadly, we lost the baby a month later.

MISCARRIAGE PART 1
August 16, 2016

I'm feeling a lot of anger right now
I want to be positive, but I don't know how
Are you healthy? Are you sick?
Will you leave? Will you stick?
If you stay, will you be OK?
No one seems to know the answer, it's all gray
I just want you to know I truly love you
I wish there was more I could do
I'll make such a nice life for you with me
But maybe here isn't where you should be
Please don't be disappointed in the choice
Please don't think you don't have a voice
I think about you and all I can give
I truly do want you to live
But sometimes life doesn't go according to a plan
And in this case G-d will have the upper hand
I'm so sorry for all of this
I wish I could make it better with a kiss.

Story behind the poem

This is such a painful poem for me. I lost a baby girl on August 19, 2016, at seventeen weeks pregnant. The process of trying to figure out if she was healthy or if she was sick was traumatizing. Over the course of the seventeen-week pregnancy, I had about seven ultrasounds and seven different doctors. I started bleeding early in the pregnancy and then the ultrasounds kept showing that the baby wasn't growing at a normal rate. But since I had a different doctor each time, they all told me I was fine and that my due date was just later than they originally thought. The doctors were rude, dismissive and made me uncomfortable. I could sense something was wrong. I knew when I had sex and I knew that Martin didn't have magic sperm that lasted forever so each time a doctor pushed back the due date, I questioned them. Plus, I had a healthy pregnancy with Dylan and intuitively knew this pregnancy wasn't going along the same trajectory. I just wanted to know if the baby, who was conceived in love, was healthy and the doctors I saw couldn't give me a straight answer. I was going crazy. I wrote this poem two days before I found out definitively from a lovely, patient high-risk doctor that it wasn't a viable pregnancy. The baby had triploidy, a rare chromosomal problem where the baby has three sets of chromosomes instead of two. Bottom line, you must be your own advocate when it comes to your health, and you have to follow your mother's intuition. Losing a baby so far along is painful enough so being tossed around the healthcare system until finally finding a competent doctor just made things worse. I'm not sure I will ever recover from this experience.

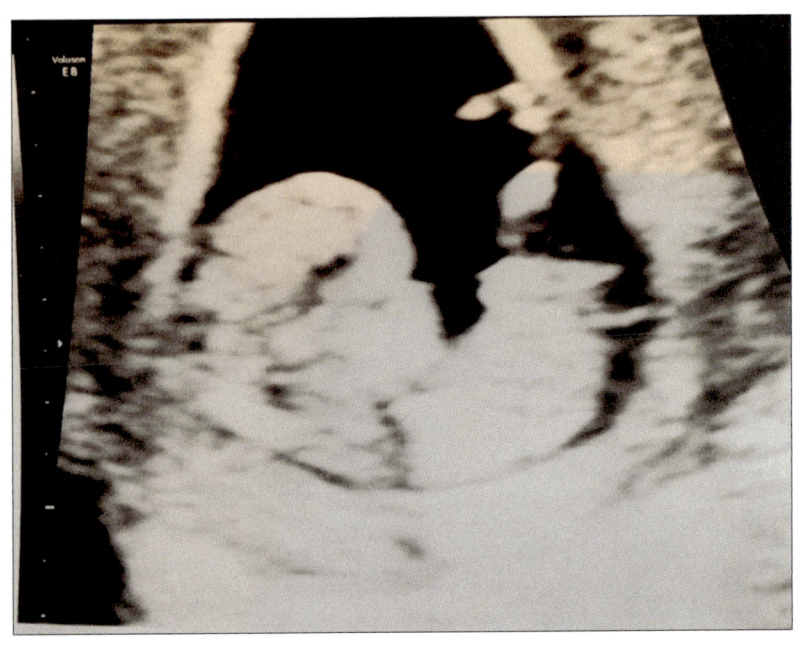

The only picture I have of the baby girl I lost.

MISCARRIAGE PART 2
August 18, 2016

Dear baby girl, tomorrow we say goodbye for good
If I could make it any other way I would
You stopped growing inside of me
And now I have to set you free
I'm sorry, I feel so guilty and sad
Already missing the baby girl I never had
I saw your fingers, legs and arms, memories I will always keep
Please forgive me, I will always think of you. Please G-d, one day we'll meet.

Story behind the poem

On August 19, 2016, I had a procedure called dilation and evacuation or D&E to remove the seventeen- week-old baby girl who stopped growing inside of me. As I sit here now, it is September 19, 2016, so it's been exactly one month. I am still healing. In the first few days after the procedure, waking up and still looking pregnant and not actually having a baby inside me was like a knife to my heart. It is still so unsettling that this wanted pregnancy and unfortunate loss is woven into the fabric of my life story. From now on, every time a doctor asks me, "How many times have you been pregnant?" and "How many children do you have?" my numbers will never add up. That is a hard reality to accept. Everyone keeps saying things to make me feel better like, "It happened for a reason," and "You will have another baby soon and you won't even think about this." Even if that is true, it doesn't make me feel better.

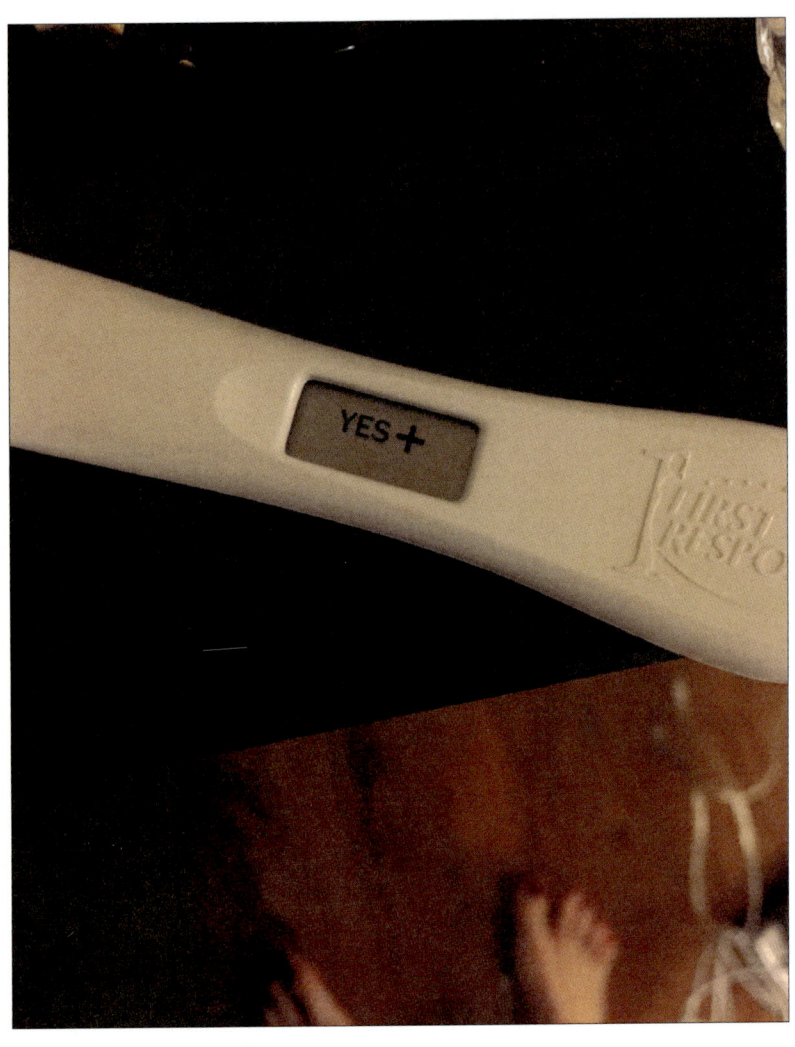

I texted Martin this photo while he was at work. Sadly, by the time of the ultrasound, we'd lost the baby.

NEW NEWS
October 2016

Hello baby, are you there, is it true
Is something growing, healthy and new
I know it's early to say I love you because we've only known each other a few hours
But for the record, I'm grateful for your presence, thank you for blessing me with your powers.

Story behind the poem
Sadly, this was not a viable pregnancy either. I found out on November 19 that I had a "normal miscarriage" this time. In 2016, I lost two babies. But this poem does capture how exciting it is to read that first positive pregnancy test and imagine the adventure that awaits.

A photo I took at a park in Philadelphia with Dylan around the time of the miscarriage.

WHAT COMES AFTER THE WORST
November 23, 2016

I am going through the motions like everything is OK
Wake up, shower, get ready for the day
But inside nothing feels normal or right
There was a spark, a flicker, that never came to light
I truly didn't see this coming, I had no way to prepare
I thought I'd hear a heartbeat, but it just wasn't there
Where do we go from here, what comes after the worst
Will someone please help me break this repetitive curse
I'm grateful for what I have, more so than before
But that doesn't really ease the pain of wanting a little more.

Story behind the poem

I wrote this poem the day before my second D&E. I hear so many stories of miscarriages and they all suck. Just a few months after losing a baby at seventeen weeks along, I was pleasantly surprised to find out I was pregnant again. I went to a new doctor for my first ultrasound and forced Martin to come along since he couldn't go to any ultrasounds during the previous pregnancy. It didn't even cross our minds that I could have another miscarriage or complication. But sure enough, there was no heartbeat. I was in shock. How could it happen again? My second D&E was November 24, 2016. My second son, Owen, was born November 24, 2017.

A photo I took when Martin proposed during a hike in Maine in 2007.

TOTALLY UNDONE
December 2016

Who am I, what have I become
I'm so lost, unraveled, undone
I can't stop obsessing, I'm running, but I'm stuck
Totally destroyed by this bad luck
I need help, but from who
Maybe a magician with a lot of glue
I'm trapped in a car that's not moving
I'm playing the game, but always losing
I have no energy, no peace, but I do have my son
Thank G-d for him, in that sense I've won.

Story behind the poem
Losing two babies within months of each other took a huge toll on me. I wrote this poem sitting in my car at a gas station too paralyzed to move. I hadn't even finished mourning the loss of my first baby girl and then I found out I was pregnant again and miscarried again. It was too much. I just kept thinking, Thank G-d I have a healthy son.

A photo of me on air at QVC on February 4. Makeup and lights can hide a lot.

BIRTHDAY
February 3, 2017

I wasn't meant to be going to work tonight
I was supposed to be rocking you and holding you tight
Instead, I'm curling my lashes and blow-drying my hair
Moving on as if you were never there
How did this happen? Why is this the truth?
I'm sorry, I'm lost. Aged before my youth
In another reality you would be with me
We'd be a family of four not three
I'm missing the little girl I never knew
But every year, on this day, I will honor you.

Story behind the poem

My due date with my little girl was February 3 but I lost her on August 19. Instead of being in labor or relishing in my new baby's smell, I was trying to get through this grueling workday, look presentable and pretend everything was normal. I remember a colleague at work, who I really like but didn't know that well, asked me if I was OK, and I just told her everything. She was lovely and comforting and just what I needed.

This photo was taken while I was pregnant with my daughter, Danika Lily. Owen was almost three and he fell asleep on my belly.

THE HAND I NEVER HELD
March 2017

Today I grieve for the hand I never held
The cry I never comforted
The laugh I never loved
I lost two little girls in one year
And with this new pregnancy I'm wracked with fear
People say having another child will help me move on
But it feels callous to just replace the ones that are gone
I'm grateful to be growing a new life inside
I pray it's drawing strength from its sisters who died.

Story behind the poem
In March 2017 I found out I was pregnant again. I had a good feeling I was going to get pregnant because I had an ultrasound on February 22, to make sure there was no scar tissue left in my uterus after my second D&E and the doctor said I was fine. He actually showed me the egg that was getting ready to leave my ovary and said that if I had sex in seven days I would get pregnant. Before the appointment, I wasn't sure I was ready to have another baby. I might have been physically healthy but mentally I wasn't. But when I saw that egg, I thought, I want that baby. I felt like just letting that egg turn into a period would be wrong. But as the pregnancy progressed, especially in the beginning, I was wracked with fear. Would I lose the baby, would the baby be healthy, would I be OK?

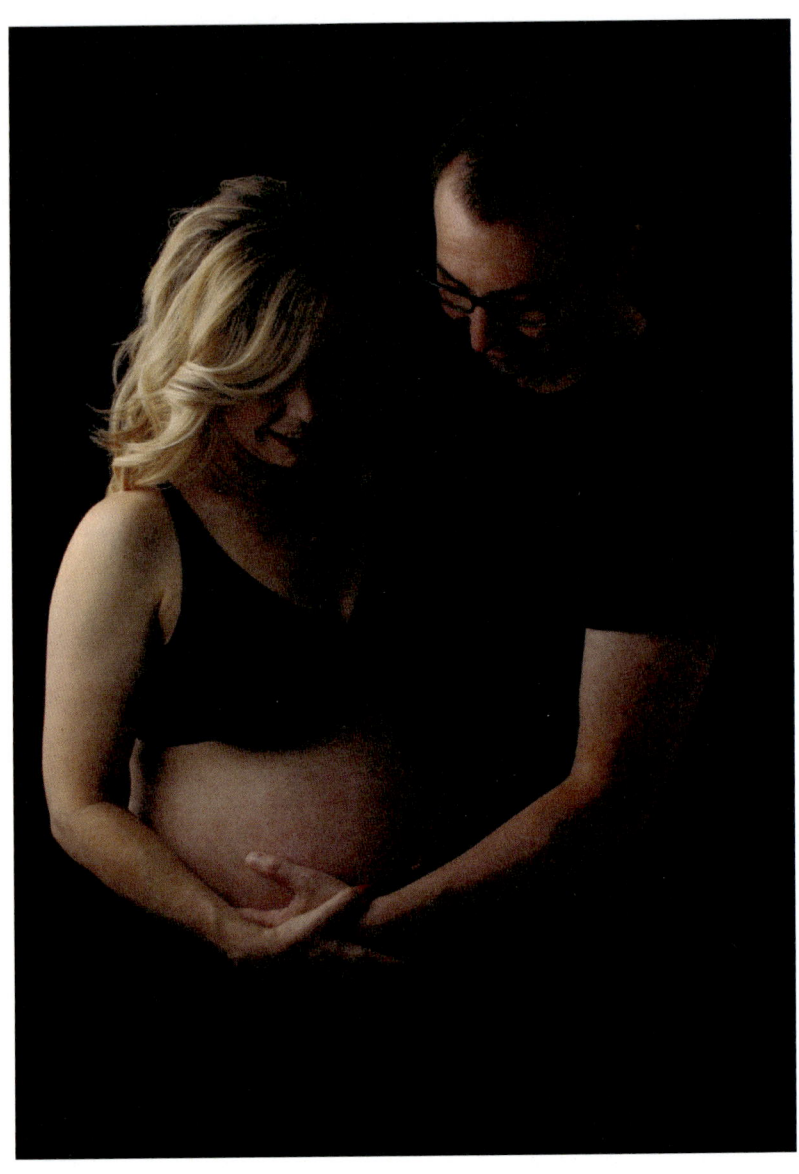

Baby Owen arrived one month after this photo was taken.

A YEAR LATER
August 19, 2017

Exactly one year ago, I lost a baby girl,
But today I wait to bring her baby brother into the world
I feel him kick and punch and stir
Feelings I never experienced with her
I still miss the daughter I'll never hold
But things happen for a reason I'm constantly told
Please G-d, bless this son so he can be a man
Give him health and strength and love in every way you can.

Story behind the poem
I am in a much better place today than I was for most of the year. Last year, I was in the hospital suffering the loss of a wanted baby, but today, I am lying on the couch with my husband, listening to my son singing songs on his guitar, rubbing my growing belly. I am due in November with a baby boy. Today we all went on a rowboat and out for ice cream and had an amazing day. This month, we moved to a new house, my husband started a new job, and we are all getting adjusted to our new life. It's amazing what a new year can bring. I am still scarred by last year and probably always will be, but I'm grateful for this moment, this new day and this baby on the way.

Pregnancy

The photo below is of me at four months pregnant with Dylan, while we were in our hotel room in the south of France. I look taken off guard, which is sort of how I felt all nine months.

INTRODUCING PREGNANCY
June 20, 2013

Whatever happens to me, happens to you
From now on we're stuck like glue
I hope it's not too bumpy of a ride
I'll do my best to take the experience in stride
I'm so excited for this change
But I must admit my body and mind feel so strange
I'm super emotional right now
And I already feel like a fat cow
I cry at practically everything I see
And I'm super worried about how often I'll pee
For thirty years, I was the only one affected by what I did
Now each decision will directly impact my kid
Hey buddy, just try to hang on tight
And I'll promise to do everything just right
Please be healthy, happy and strong
And I'll protect you and love you forever long.

Story behind the poem
Pregnancy was a bit traumatic for me. I basically vomited for nine months straight with all three. I even vomited throughout the labors, which is why I only needed to push three times each. It's bizarre and amazing and worthwhile in every way. I pray that every woman who wants to be pregnant, has the opportunity.

My friend Andrew from In Touch Weekly *took this photo in January 2014. It hangs in my bedroom.*

MY LITTLE SEED
October 29, 2013

Dear baby, you are the precious seed growing inside me
What your dad and I started, the world has yet to see
I imagine holding you in my arms and feeling your soft skin
Experiencing my heart melt every time you grin
I picture driving you to school and cooking each meal
Listening to you laugh or helping you heal
May you travel the world and explore new things
May you find true love and all the joy it brings
As you cycle through life, you'll make choices of your own
And I'll think back to when you were my little seed and marvel how you've grown
Thank you for letting me be your mom, it's the best gift by far
You are my angel, my world, my beautiful star.

Story behind the poem
I remember writing this and envisioning reading this to my son on his wedding day. I tear up just thinking about it. I feel like he would be very embarrassed if I read this in public so I might just read it to him in private. The journey of life is so miraculous.

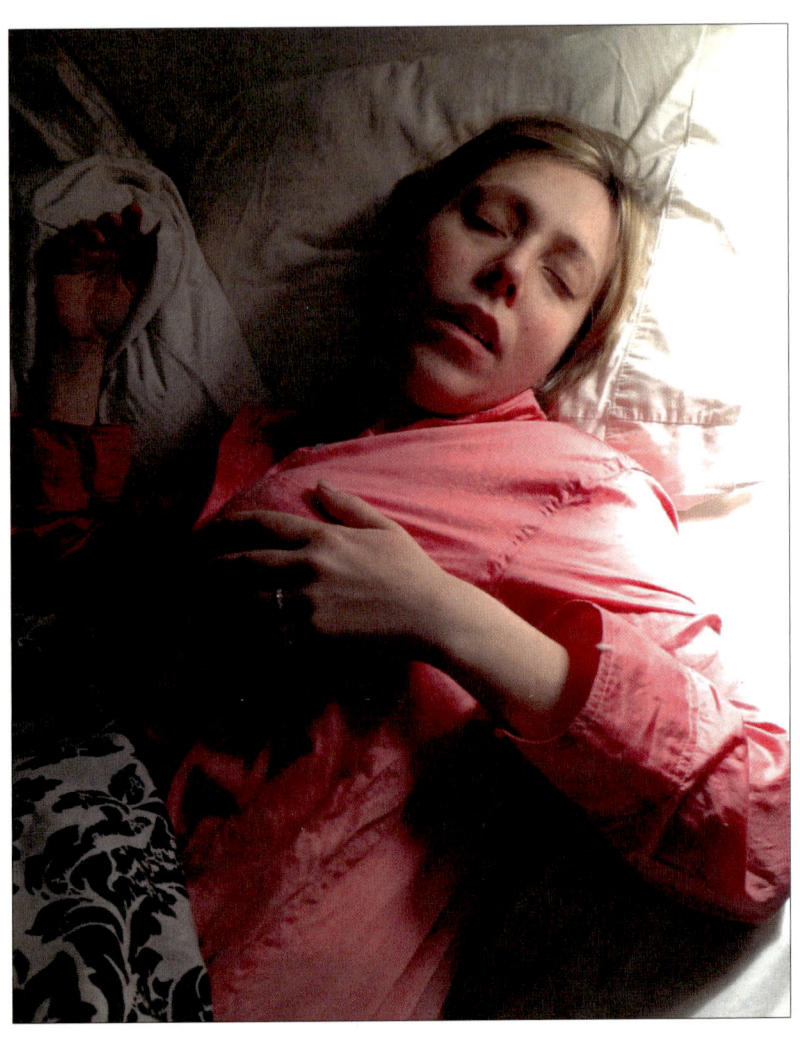

I just love how protective I am over my engorged breasts, even in my sleep.

THE DOWNSIDE OF PREGNANCY
August 29, 2013

Pregnancy has not been an easy ride
I feel so fat all I want to do is hide
I am not experiencing that pregnancy glow
All I have is acne to show
I'm still nauseous and super bloated
And with dark hairs I'm coated
How big am I going to get
What else can I expect
I wish I had a map all laid out
Maybe then I wouldn't feel the urge to scream and shout.

Story behind the poem
I had rough pregnancies. Maybe I wasn't Kate Middleton sick, but I could do without the vomiting LIVE on air during an hour show at QVC, throwing up on the F train and spending a Thanksgiving hooked up to an IV. Nevertheless, the fuss was beyond worth it.

My attempt at being "pregnancy sexy" while carrying baby Danika in August 2020.

THE UPSIDE OF PREGNANCY
November 21, 2013

Dear baby, I wake up to kicking from your little feet
Feeling you inside me is the biggest treat
Even bad days are better because of you,
When I'm stressed out or sad, you turn gray skies blue
I think about you swimming around
Drinking and eating, growing pound by pound
My little bundle of joy
My precious baby boy
Keep cooking until you are ready to come out
We can't wait to see what all the fuss was about.

Story behind the poem
I love this poem because as sick as I felt during pregnancy, this shows that I didn't lose sight of the miracle happening. But I did throw up right after writing this, for the record!

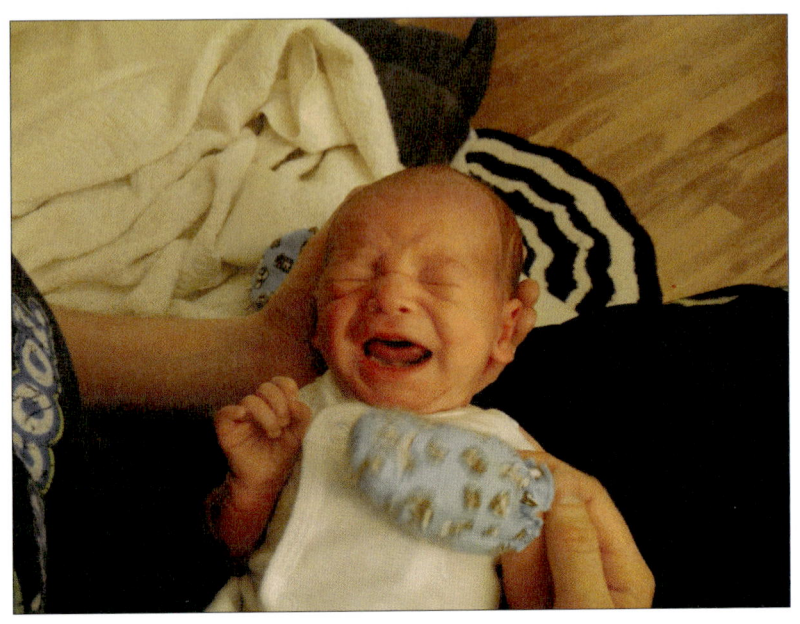

Here is an example of Dylan at just five days old hysterical and we had no clue what to do!

MOTHERING ON A PRAYER
November 20, 2013

What if I don't know how to get the baby to stop crying?
How often do I cut his nails, if I told you I knew, I'd be lying
When do I feed him, when does he nap?
What if I get sick cleaning up his crap?
What if I drop him or accidentally hit his head?
What if he is never tired and refuses to go to bed?
What if I suck at being a mom,
And can't figure out anything and totally bomb?
I'm scared and hope this little guy will be OK,
Otherwise, what do I do, I guess I'll just pray.

Story behind this poem
I am smiling as I read this poem because most of the things I was concerned about actually happened with baby Dylan. I still struggle to cut his nails, I gagged cleaning up his poop, he accidentally rolled off the bed when he was about nine months (he was fine, but I was traumatized) and he has gone through countless phases of refusing to sleep. And in all those moments, I've just taken a deep breath and prayed. I guess that is the best advice I can give new moms: Shit happens, literally and figuratively, so learn how to pray.

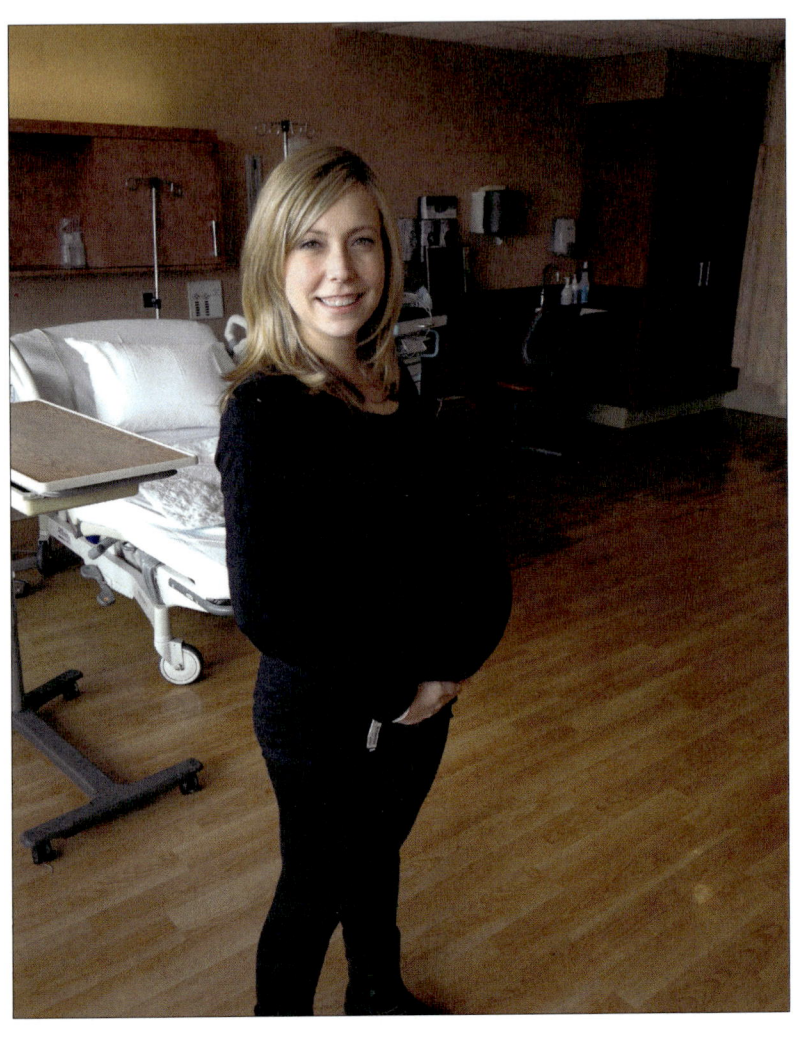

Photo of me right before Dylan's birth. I was naively calm.

KABOOM
January 18, 2014

I feel like a ticking time bomb
Not sure when I'm going to go
Hoping I don't detonate too soon
Praying I'll be clued in enough to know
I wonder if I'll explode at night
Or during the clarity of daylight
Will I be alone or with your dad
Will I be scared or infinitely glad
Will you take a while to make your entrance
Or will you break through like a bull clearing a fence
Will I scream or welcome you with laughter
Will it be a smooth blow or a shaky disaster
I know the countdown has already begun
Here's hoping the aftermath will be a barrel of fun.

Story behind the poem
I was due February 24, 2014 and gave birth to Dylan February 26. The pregnancy was rough but thankfully, the delivery was manageable. Honestly, I think getting dental work is worse than pushing out a baby, but that is just my experience. Many of my friends feel otherwise and rightly so.

Pregnant with Owen heading to Rosh Hashana services.

SOMETHING NEW
September 26, 2017

I already love you even though we haven't met face-to-face
I'll miss feeling you inside me, but I'm excited for you to have your own space
This is really happening. Soon I will be a mom again
I'm nervous and thrilled. I'd love to know exactly when
My bonus baby, my second son
Not even here yet and I feel I've already won.

Story behind the poem
I am so relieved I wrote this poem. When I was pregnant with Dylan it seems like poems and emotions were pouring out of me. But being that I was so traumatized by my two miscarriages, I feel like I didn't relish my pregnancy with Owen enough. Owen was born November 24, exactly a year to the day of my second miscarriage.

First professional photo of Danika Lily. She is a natural!

WORTHWHILE
December 19, 2013

Who was I before I starting making you
Now you're a part of everything I do
From the moment I get out of bed
To the second I rest my head
I'm committed to your protection
Making sure we're going in the right direction
I only want the best for you
You give worth to everything I do.

Story behind the poem
I wrote this poem a few months before Dylan was born. I think I really captured what it truly means for me to be a mom. Dylan, Owen and now Danika, give worth to everything I do. Before becoming a mom, I identified myself through my career and my weight. Now, my kids are my priority. They also make me a better person. Because of them, I want to do more, create more, and just be the best version of myself.

Relationships and Marriage

Photo of us on our honeymoon in Santorini, Greece, 2010.

MARTIN
October 10, 2012

I crave his company and feel at peace in his arms
I'm appeased by his genuine charms

The greatest joy is making him laugh
He is by far my better half

When he isn't around I feel amiss
Being together is pure bliss

For my husband I will always pine
I am so thankful he is mine.

Story behind the poem

This sounds like a country song to me with the lyric "I crave his company." I do crave my husband's company and I am often a little lost when he isn't around. I am an independent person, but I feel lucky that I don't always have to be. Ironically, this was written at the height of my parent's divorce. They separated for the first time right after Martin and I got married in 2010, after forty-one years together. Then ended up getting back together for a few years but divorced again in 2018. It's a long story!

Wedding photo May 30, 2010.

BLENDED
May 7, 2013

There is nothing I love more than when our bodies entwine
When I can't tell the difference between your limbs and mine
Or when our hands clasp in the middle of the night
Even our subconscious knows togetherness is right
With just one embrace and all is mended
You and I truly belong blended.

Story behind the poem
I wrote this around the time of our three-year wedding anniversary. And the words still ring true to me every day. I believe Martin and I are the best versions of ourselves when we are together. I feel less stressed, more capable and confident when he is around. I remember when my sister, Ali, gave her speech at our wedding she said, "Martin calms Amy down and Amy makes Martin smile." We are so lucky to have each other.

Our first date, the night that started it all.

AMERICAN IDOL SONG: AS I GO AWAY
May 2007

We've been together so long, but far apart at the same time
Now you're asking me to change, where do I draw the line?
Moving across country to be closer to you
Means I'll have to give up my life now and start something new,
Is that bad, is that good, I just don't know
But ten years down the road, what if I wish I didn't go

Chorus: You mean the world to me, but maybe that's too much
             I love your kiss, your scent, your touch
             But how can I survive relying on such.

I have plans to write a book,
Learn how to dance, maybe even cook
I also dream of starring in a play
Traveling the world, and becoming famous one day
I planned on accomplishing these things on my own
I figured that's the upside of being alone
Then I met you and fell in love fast
Who knew a childhood crush like ours could last

Chorus: You mean the world to me, but maybe that's too much
              I love your kiss, your scent, your touch
             But how can I survive relying on such.

You're asking me to change my ways
Without a guarantee my sacrifices will bring better days
I love you for including me in your dream
But what if mine rips at the seam
I don't blame you for these little earthquakes
I'm just afraid you might be the only one standing after my world breaks

Chorus:	You mean the world to me, but maybe that's too much
	I love your kiss, your scent, your touch
	But how can I survive relying on such.

You have your own destiny to find
And I don't want to be left behind
Is there a solution for us to stay together
Because I don't want to live without you forever
Stay positive, that's what they say
So I'll keep that in mind as I go away

Chorus:	You mean the world to me, and baby, that's enough
	I love your kiss, your scent, your touch
	And I know I can survive relying on such

Story behind the poem:
I wrote this poem in May 2007. My boyfriend, who is now my husband, Martin, got into medical school in NYC, but I was making a name for myself at E! News in LA as an associate producer. So I really struggled with whether or not to move. But as the last verse explains, I did move (thankfully E! News said I could transfer to the Manhattan office), and things worked out better than expected. But what really inspired me to write this poem was after I heard American Idol was holding a song-writing contest. I remember sitting at my tiny desk in my studio apartment and writing these words. Ironically, I thought that eight hundred square foot apartment was tiny, but once I actually did move to New York later that month, I had a whole new appreciation for that LA studio. Unfortunately, American Idol wouldn't accept just the lyrics, because they wanted the melody too, and since I am tone-deaf, that put an end to my dream of winning the contest. But I did write a beautiful love song so if anyone out there can sing and knows music, contact me!

SIDE NOTE: Ironically, in 2004, I did work at American Idol. And when I say "work," I mean I was a page for CBS and American Idol filmed on CBS's lot. So my job was to seat the audience members and carry around a plastic cup and ask them to spit their chewing gum into it because there was no chewing gum allowed on set. I wore a red blazer with moth holes from the seventies with a gray bow tie. And to make the experience even more humbling, I was actually working the night Carrie Underwood won. I remember standing at my post near a trash can, looking up at her and thinking, I graduated from Emory University with highest honors and my life has led me to collecting chewed gum from strangers and this girl is actually a year younger than me. Life is not fair. But again, it all worked out. Wouldn't it be full circle if Carrie ended up singing this song? Please, universe, help me make this so. I interviewed her once at New York Fashion Week. She was lovely and has the most amazing legs ever! I also knew her stylist back in the day when I was a fashion editor for In Touch Weekly. So who knows, maybe we are destined to work together!

Martin and me at Keukenhof Gardens in the Netherlands in 2013.

AFTER I DO
September 21, 2010

Since getting married, I never felt more single
I find myself alone a lot, with no one to mingle
I often pick up dinner for one instead of two
I fantasize about what it would be like to hold you
And despite the detachment, no resentment do I feel
I knew what I was getting into when I signed the deal.

Story behind the poem
I wrote this story just four months after our wedding and a few months into my husband's first year of his residency program. Over the years, my feelings have changed. I love my husband more than ever and am very proud of his accomplishments, but I miss him, and to be honest, I am sometimes resentful that he isn't always around when I need him. He is such an amazing dad, husband and my best friend. I am grateful, though, that I have my own job and hobbies. I think it's important.

The night of Martin's fellowship graduation. He got called in to work as the dinner started and missed it.

THE DOCTOR'S WIFE
February 2017

I am trying to think of something nice you've done for me
But really all I'm coming up with is empty
Sure there was a dinner here or there
But I usually initiated and you didn't really care
I lost so much this year and I've struggled to recover
But what I miss the most is the connection with my lover
You used to make me feel invincible
Now-a-days it seems I'm just invisible
When did I lose my stature, when did my needs get pushed aside
I've got to be honest, I don't have the will anymore to hide
I am a woman, a mother, a daughter, a friend and a wife
But if you can't recognize this, it's time to get out of my life.

Story behind the poem

Twenty sixteen was a brutal year for me. Martin was doing his fellowship and I hardly ever saw him. Plus, I miscarried twice, and he wasn't really there for any of it. I felt so alone and resentful. I remember one afternoon I was recovering from a bad stomach virus and a very exhausting workweek. Martin was finally home and he, Dylan and I were all in the basement. Martin was holding me, and we were watching Dylan play and I just started crying. I was crying over losing two babies, I was crying because I was tired and because I felt so alone. I was pretty hysterical, but trying to calm down since I knew Martin was there when all of a sudden his phone rang and he was called in to work. Someone was having a stroke. He just left me there, crying. For anyone who has had a loved one go through the stages of becoming a doctor, you know it's tough on everyone. But the fellowship years, compounded by the fact that I had lost two babies, was raising our son and working crazy hours at QVC made life so challenging. I think the hardest part for both Martin and me was that we love each other. In theory, I knew he wanted to be with me, but in reality, he wasn't.

We took a quick trip to Florida in 2007. A man on the beach took this photo. We were so happy in this moment. I love this photo!

LONG DISTANCE
January 2006

I listen to you speak and imagine our life together
A house, a few kids, and in love forever
I hear your dreams as you share your thoughts for a while
A life of bliss, extravagance and style
The sound of your voice is full of comfort and care
But when I reach out to hold you, no one is there
The chorus stops playing, the composer has gone away
Silence lingers and there are no words left to say
I long for an encore, one last note, please abide
Without your song, I'm just empty inside
I want to record every lyric and remember every key
Something to pass the time until you come back to me.

Story behind the poem
Martin and I spent three years doing long distance and it was painful. We spoke on the phone regularly and visited each other as often as we could. He was in medical school in New York and I was in Los Angeles at E! News. Those phones calls kept us going. As I sit here in our house full of children, I am grateful we succeeded at a long-distance relationship.

Dylan took this photo of us in LA around the time of the fight. We look happy in this picture though.

CAN'T RELATE
November 2018

Was the laughter only in my head
Did we once sleep in the same bed
I am still obsessing about the fight the night before
But I doubt you are thinking about it anymore
You are going about your day
Basically hoping I won't get in your way
I worry, I cry, I stay up too late
That's who I am, and I guess you can't relate.

Story behind the poem
After a fight between Martin and me, I can spend hours thinking about it and analyzing every word with my girlfriends. But not Martin, he can just get up shower and start a new day. Or at least that is how it feels to me.

Family of four photo from August 2019. A year or so later we became a family of five.

DIVORCE
December 25, 2018

What kind of relationship do my kids see
When they look at their father and me
Do they think we are happy or always mad
Can they tell when I am hurt by their dad
Will they remember the laughter over the fights
Will they forget any sleepless nights
I tried not to copy my parents' choices
I can't stand the anger in their voices
I believe I picked the right partner and friend
I really want our union to last until the end
Setting a good example of what marriage can be is my goal
I want my kids to know there is a perfect half to make them feel whole
As long as they see love is the foundation of their parents' relationship
And accept that sometimes we lose our balance and trip
Then I've done my job as a mother and a wife
To teach my kids marriage can be for life.

Story behind the poem

I wrote this around the time my parents were getting divorced for a second time. Even though I was an adult by the time their marriage dissolved, the experience took a toll on me. To be honest, I think they are probably happier apart than together, but that's not how I feel about my life with Martin. I want my kids to know a marriage can last forever. I hope mine does.

This photo was taken the day before I wrote the poem. Martin was working on a weekend again, so I took my kids to a hayride. He eventually met us there.

LEAVES ME BITTER
October 27, 2021

Is it easy for you to leave
Once you're gone do you even grieve
Do we ever cross your mind
Or are we a memory you prefer not find
What's it like to just sit there
Alone, at ease, with no care
My voice hurts from screaming
My chest throbs from breathing
My heart breaks
My back aches
I want to give up too
I want to leave just like you
But we can't both be the quitter
So I guess that just leaves me bitter.

Story behind the poem

I wrote this while I was putting my son Owen to bed. He was playing with dinosaurs on the floor and before we started reading books, I was inspired to put these words down. My husband had left for a medical conference in Las Vegas earlier in the week. In all honesty, I was feeling lonely and jealous that he got to go away, and I was stuck putting the kids to bed for three nights straight by myself. I just pictured him sitting on an airplane with a drink in his hand staring out the window. But I also feel this poem captures how parents going through a divorce might feel. I played a lot with the word "leave." This is another instance when I would love for this poem to become a country song. Kelly Clarkson, are you available?

Dylan took this photo of us on a trip to Washington, D.C. in 2019.

LITTLE SURPRISES
January 19, 2019

After all these years you still surprise me
It's the little things that make me so happy
In a time when our life feels a mess
With one gesture you wipe away the stress
I know loving me must be tough
So thank you, I realize I don't say it enough.

Story behind the poem
Out of nowhere, Martin will do little things like buy me flowers if I had a bad day or surprise me in ways I think he would kill me if I shared. We started dating as sophomores in college and now we are forty. I am just so touched that he still cares, and for the record, I do surprise him too!

CONCLUSION

Thank you for taking this journey with me. I hope you feel comforted knowing you are not alone. I have more to share, so stay in touch.

ABOUT THE AUTHOR

Amy Oselkin is a QVC on-air guest host for Clarks Shoes. Previously, she was the senior lifestyle editor at *In Touch Weekly*. She also worked as a bicoastal reporter for *E! News*. She was born and raised in Los Angeles before attending Emory University in Atlanta, where she double majored in journalism and theater studies. She now lives with her husband, two boys and baby girl in Allentown, Pennsylvania.

Made in the USA
Las Vegas, NV
07 May 2023